BYGONE TIMES

&

A SASH MY GRANDFATHER WORE

By

Brian McConnell

Front cover photo of Sash of Sir Knight of the Royal Black Knights

of Grand Black Chapter of British America

Copyright © 2022 Brian McConnell

ISBN: 9798801449555

CONTENTS

1. INTRODUCTION

During the course of doing family research some twenty years ago I obtained a Report of the Proceedings of the Grand Black Chapter of Ireland held December, 1907 and June 1908. In it I found listed the name of my great uncle James Arnold.   He lived in Ballybay, County Monaghan, Ireland.   His name was listed as the Master (or Preceptor) of Royal Black Preceptory No. 218, which was called "Rising Sons of Ballybay".

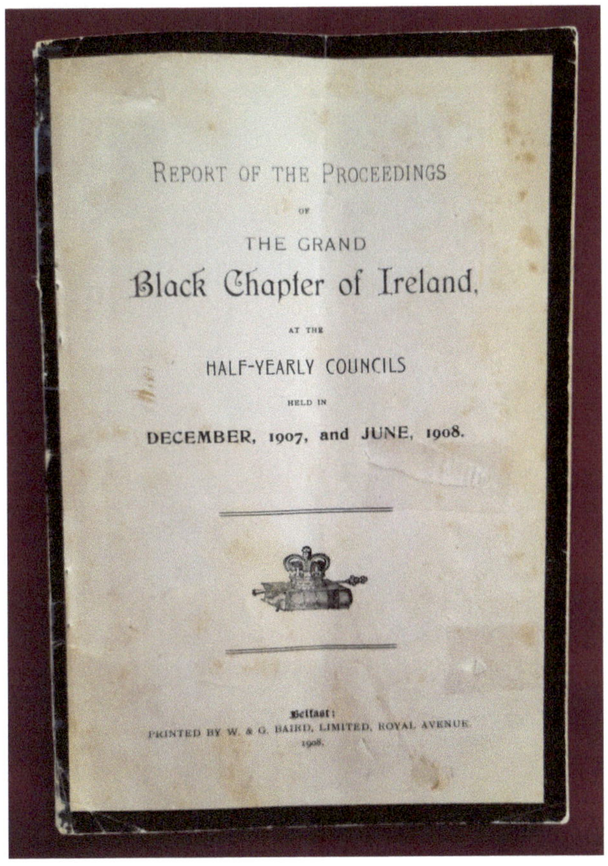

Finding this information encouraged me to go further in my research. I learned that my grandfather after he immigrated to Canada from Ireland was also a Royal Black Knight.

This short book contains a description of the type of Sash that was worn by members of the Royal Black Institution. It also includes a listing of the Preceptories in Canada as appeared in the 1960 Report of Proceedings of the Imperial Grand Black Chapter of the British Commonwealth, with their location and name of Preceptor and address.

It is my goal in publishing this book to share information with others who may inquire about a relative that was a member of the Royal Black Institution and to provide this as a resource.

Brian McConnell

April 14, 2022

2. THE SASH

As people interested in genealogy or family history try to learn about past relatives they sometimes inquire about old regalia they find and are unfamiliar with like a sash their grandfather may have worn of a Royal Black Knight. I was contacted by a museum in New Brunswick and asked to give information about an old sash similar to the one in the picture below. It is a sash worn by a Royal Black Knight. Royal Black Knights were members of the Royal Black Institution, a Protestant fraternal association formed in Ireland in 1797 that spread to Canada. (1)

By the late 1800s the association was present in all provinces of Canada. It organized as the Grand Black Chapter of British America and was affiliated with the Loyal Orange Association in Canada . (2)

In addition to promotion of the Protestant faith all branches of the Loyal Orange Association supported the British Monarchy and links to the Commonwealth.   Canada's first Prime Minister, Sir. John A. Macdonald, was an Orangeman as was the last Father of Confederation, Premier Joseph Smallwood of Newfoundland, along with many other leaders including Tommy Douglas, seventh Premier of Saskatchewan, the first leader of the New Democratic Party, who is known as the Father of Medicare. Dominic Di Stasi, son of an Italian immigrant, Grand Master of the Grand Orange Lodge in Canada from 1994 to 1996 belonged to Giuseppe Garibaldi Loyal Orange Lodge No. 3115 in Toronto whose members were mostly from the Protestant Italian community.(3)   Oronhyateka, Mohawk physician and scholar born on the Six Nations of the Grand River near Brantford was an Orangeman and County Master of Middlesex. (4) There were several Orange lodges of which the members were First Nations people including Loyal Orange Lodge No. 99, the last active Mohawk lodge which was located on the Reservation at Deseronto, Ontario. (5) The size of the membership declined in the twentieth century and dramatically after World Ward II. Royal Black Knights now are found mainly in southern Ontario and Newfoundland. Labrador.

The sash pictured in this article is over 100 years old. On it are emblems associated with the 11 degrees in the Royal Black Institution. The 11 degrees, based on stories in the Bible are taught to members. Each member belonged to a local lodge known as a Royal Black Preceptory where he could earn degrees.   The names of the degrees are: 1) Royal

Black; 2) Royal Scarlet; 3) Royal Mark; 4) Apron and Royal Blue; 5) Royal White; 6) Royal Green; 7) Royal Gold; 8) Star and Garter; 9) Order of the Crimson Arrow; 10) Order of the Link and Chain; 11) Order of the Red Cross.

The photo of the sash below shows the lettering 'RBP 519" which stands for Royal Black Preceptory No. 519 which was located at New Glasgow, Nova Scotia.(6) In 1959 there were over 350 Preceptories across Canada and 12 were active in Nova Scotia. These were: No. 117 called *Johnston* in Halifax with Worshipful Preceptor S. Messervery; No. 294, in Springhill led by Burton Vance; No. 341, *Inniskilling*, in North Sydney, with William Lowe; No. 358, *Golden Star*, in Glace Bay, with A.A. Stevenson; No. 519, *Rising Sun*, in New Glasgow, with James Rodgers; No. 567, *Edward VII* in Westville; No. 678 *Iron City,* in Whitney Pier (Sydney) with Paul W. Skanes; No. 865, *Sceptre*, in Lunenburg, with E.H. Miller; No. 1245, in New Aberdeen, Cape Breton, with Herbert Chant; and No. 1275, *Alexander McIntosh*, in Richmond, with Theodore Fisher. See Appendix A for a listing of all warrants to Royal Black Preceptories in Canada as of 1959.

A sash like the one pictured was worn by the member to meetings of the Preceptory and functions associated with it like church services, parades or funerals of other members.   On Sunday, November 3, 1929 in St. James Presbyterian Church at Truro, Nova Scotia a church service was held with the Black Knights and the Loyal Orange Association led by Reverend C. Ritchie Bell as Minister.   The Order of Service and Notes appear in Appendix B.

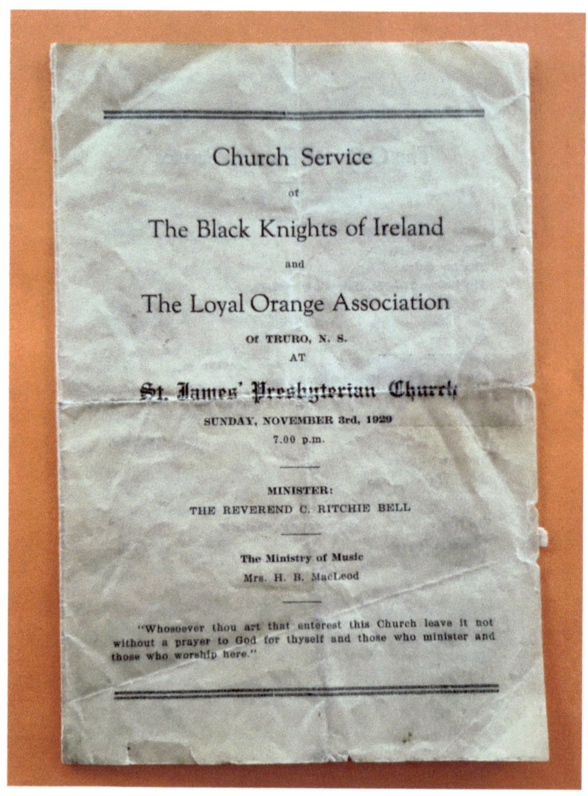

Church Service

of

The Black Knights of Ireland

and

The Loyal Orange Association

Of TRURO, N. S.

AT

St. James' Presbyterian Church

SUNDAY, NOVEMBER 3rd, 1929

7.00 p.m.

MINISTER:

THE REVEREND C. RITCHIE BELL

The Ministry of Music

Mrs. H. B. MacLeod

"Whosoever thou art that enterest this Church leave it not without a prayer to God for thyself and those who minister and those who worship here."

Pictured below is Seward Thomas Grant wearing a Royal Black Knight sash. He resided in Glace Bay, Nova Scotia and died on August 28, 1935 His sash is similar to the one pictured in this article. He is also wearing an apron which Royal Black Knights could wear similar to those worn by Masons in Masonic Lodges. On his lower arms and wrists are cuffs of a type sometimes worn by Officers in the Preceptory. When wearing this regalia members dressed in their finest clothes as if they were going to church. Members were called Sir Knights.

Preceptories varied in size but most were between 15 and 30 members that met monthly in Orange Lodge Halls or halls of other community groups. Some met bi-monthly. All meetings of Preceptories after opening had a Scripture reading followed by repetition of the Royal Black Degree, minutes of former meeting, communications, collection of dues, reports, initiations of any new candidates, general business and advancement to higher degree by members. (7)

The Preceptory Officers elected annually included: Worshipful Preceptor, a position like President; Deputy Preceptor; Chaplain, who often was the minister from a local church; Registrar, who performed duties of a Secretary; Treasurer; 1st Lecturer and 2nd Lecturer for providing memorized lectures during ritual part of meanings; 1st Censor and 2nd Censor; 1st Standard Bearer and 2nd Standard Bearer; Pursuivant; Tyler, two Auditors and a Committee of seven members.

On the application for membership to join a Preceptory of the Royal Black Institution the applicant confirmed his date of birth, place of birth, occupation, and religious denomination. He also indicated the number of the Orange Lodge he belonged to as that was a prerequisite to joining. Pictured below is an Application completed by William J. Barrett on January 7, 1935 who applied and was accepted for membership in Royal Black Preceptory No. 358 at Glace Bay, Nova Scotia. His occupation appears as physician.

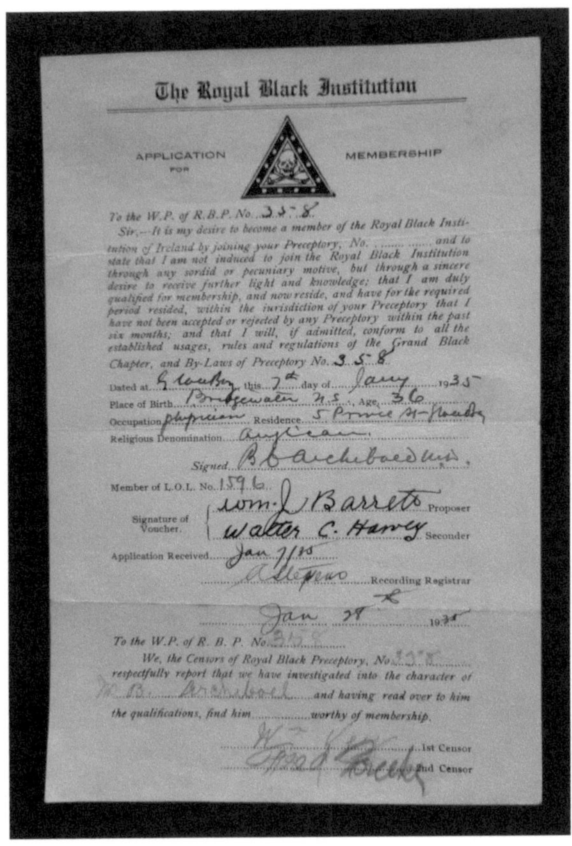

The Royal Black Institution

APPLICATION FOR   MEMBERSHIP

To the W.P. of R.B.P. No. 358

Sir,—It is my desire to become a member of the Royal Black Institution of Ireland by joining your Preceptory, No. .... and to state that I am not induced to join the Royal Black Institution through any sordid or pecuniary motive, but through a sincere desire to receive further light and knowledge; that I am duly qualified for membership, and now reside, and have for the required period resided, within the jurisdiction of your Preceptory that I have not been accepted or rejected by any Preceptory within the past six months; and that I will, if admitted, conform to all the established usages, rules and regulations of the Grand Black Chapter, and By-Laws of Preceptory No. 358.

Dated at Glauby, this 7th day of Jany, 1935

Place of Birth Bridgewater N.S., Age 36

Occupation physician   Residence 5 Prince St—Hauts

Religious Denomination Anglican.

Signed B B Archibald MD.

Member of L.O.L. No. 1596.

Signature of Voucher.   Wm. J. Barrett .... Proposer

Walter C. Harvey .... Seconder

Application Received Jan 7/35

A Stevens .... Recording Registrar

Jan 28 1935

To the W.P. of R. B. P. No. 358

We, the Censors of Royal Black Preceptory, No. 358 respectfully report that we have investigated into the character of W. B. Archibald and having read over to him the qualifications, find him .... worthy of membership.

.... 1st Censor

.... 2nd Censor

On the top of this Application is another symbol associated with the Royal Black Knights. It is the skull and cross bones. It as well as the Cross and Crown appeared on regalia sometimes as well as on caps and rings. This can be seen in an old Price List for Royal Black Knights prepared by Dominion Regalia of Toronto which is in Appendix C.

The photograph below shows a meeting of a Preceptory in Fredericton, New Brunswick in the early 1900s.

From this photograph above can be seen that in the center of the meeting room was placed a pedestal or desk upon which the Bible lay. Immediately behind this is seated the Worshipful Preceptor with the other Officers on each side.   On the walls hang pictures of the King and Queen as well as ones of notable members and certificates related to the Preceptory.

The Preceptories were organized into provincial associations which met yearly to deal with business within their jurisdictions. Ontario was divided into Ontario East and Ontario West. It had the largest number of Preceptories. The parent association, the Grand Black Chapter of British America, also held an annual session. These sessions were attended by elected national leaders of the association along with representatives of the Preceptories and other members as visitors. Each year the sessions were held in a different location.   Below is a photo of the front and back of the Proclamation for the 1960 session. It was the 86th annual session as the association was founded in Canada in 1874. This session took place at the King Edward Hotel in Toronto, Ontario.

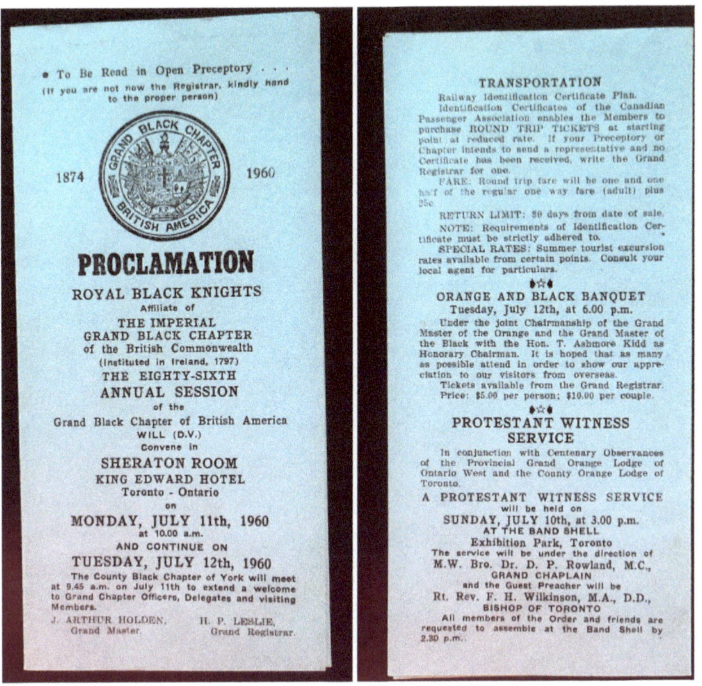

3. NOTES

(1) McConnell, Brian, "The Royal Black Knights in Canada", ISBN 9798697082041, published 2020

(2) Houston, Cecil, J, and Smyth, William, J. "The Sash Canada Wore – A Historical Geography of the Orange Order in Canada", ISBN 0802054935, Toronto; University of Toronto Press, 1980

(3) "Dominic Di Stasi – A Man Who Challenged Diversity" accessed online on April 7, 2022 at http://www.orangeontario.org/about-us/modern-times/

(4) "Oryonhatekha" in The Canadian Encyclopedia, accessed online on April 7, 2022 at
https://www.thecanadianencyclopedia.ca/en/article/oronhyatekha

(5) "Mohawks are big hit in Ulster -Deseronto Indians belong to last lodge run by natives", The (Kingston) Whig – Standard, Oct. 6, 1990, p. 1

(6) 1959 - 1960 Report of Proceedings of Imperial Grand Black Chapter of British Commonwealth

(7) The Royal Black Institution in Canada, Grand Black Chapter, Rules and Regulations, published January 1, 1999

4. APPENDIX "A"

WARRANTS WORKING UNDER THE GRAND BLACK CHAPTER OF BRITISH AMERICA, 1959

There were a total of 384 which include the following breakdown by Province: British Columbia, 8; Alberta, 6; Saskatchewan, 8; Manitoba, 11; Western Ontario, 93; Eastern Ontario, 53; New Brunswick, 13; Nova Scotia, 10; Newfoundland and Labrador, 174; Quebec, 3; and Prince Edward Island, 5.

Among the names of the Preceptories some were based on: a) the Bible, like Olive Branch, King Hiram, Calvary, Star of the West, and King Solomon; b) others British monarchs and royalty including Victoria, King Edward III, Duke of York, King George II; c) Battles such as Lundy's Lane, Vimy Ridge, Gallipoli, and Beaumont Hamel; d) connections to Ireland included Ulster, Clougher, Knights of Ulster, Friends of Ulster, and Ulster Covenant; e) Political, Religious or Lodge leaders like Johnston of Ballykilbeag, John Knox, Clark Wallace, Sir Henry Wilson, and Lord Kitchener.

Provincial Jurisdiction of British Columbia

No./ Name / Where Held / Sir Knight (Registrar) & Address

372 / Beaver / Mission City / Lea Clarke, Mission City

378 / Olive Branch / Abbotsford / J.A. McGregor, Langley

459 / Royal City / New Westminster / W.J. Campbell, 775 Shaware,

Coquitlam

538 / Victoria / Victoria / F.F. King, 1414 Craigflower Rd., Victoria

544 / Star of the West / Vancouver / H.J. Crass Weller, 7342 Curtis, North Burnaby

736 / Eldon / Coquitlam / George Steeves, 20540 Stanton St., Coquitlam

802 / Vancouver / Vancouver / N., Ferson, 3612 Franklin St., Vancouver

819 / Eldon / Princeton / G.A. Taylor, Princeton

Provincial Jurisdiction of Alberta

547 / Calgary / Calgary / L.E. McKay, 1401 3rd St. NW, Calgary

654 / Strathcona / Edmonton / H.B.Wallace, 10306 – 83rd St., Edmonton

806 / King William / Edmonton / S.P. Dickson, 12327 80th St., Edmonton

948 / Victoria / Manville / A.E. Williams, Manville

975 / Memento / Red Deer / A.L. Briers, 5313 43rd Ave., Red Deer

1205 / Wainwright / Wainright / E.F. Smith, Wainwright

Provincial Jurisdiction of Saskatchewan

581 / Pile of Bones / Regina / R.W. Sandercock, 817 Horace St., Regina

724 / Albert / Prince Albert / H.S. Winters, 147 - 13th St. W., Prince Albert

884 / Melville / Creelman / W. Henderson, Fillmore

898 / Star of the North / Tisdall / David Bleakely, Ridgedale

983 / Tisdale / Nipawin / Dudley Wright, Nipawin

1128 / Calvary / Eston / Myro L. Daley, Eston

1131 / Excelsior / Wiseton / W.J. Johnston, Rose Town, Wiseton

1297 / Moose Jaw / Moose Jaw / W.G. Knox, 1236 1st Ave., Moose Jaw

Provincial Jurisdiction of Manitoba

338 / Hamiota / Hamiota / W.W. Cochran, Hamiota

380 / Winnipeg / Winnipeg / J.E. Lucas, 29522 Main St., Winnipeg

396 / Killarney / Killarney / F.G. Grinnell, Killarney

515 / High Bluff / Portage La Prairie / George Ferguson, 143 6th St. NE,

Portage La Prairie

540 / Hartney / Hartney / W.S. Spratt, Elgin

543 / King Edward / Carman / Jack Stuary, Carman

602 / Dauphin / Dauphin / A.B. Crawford, Dauphin

685 / Eldon / Winnipeg / H.R. Sweetland, 432 Bannatyne Ave., Winnipeg

731 / Jordan / Swan River / O.S. Gold, Swan River

732 / Brandon / Brandon / J.T. Kennedy, 363 Percy St., Brandon

733 / Juniper / Winnipeg / Robert E. Clarke, 42 Pilgrim Ave., Winnipeg

Provincial Jurisdiction of Western Ontario

96 / Maiden / Toronto / David Service, 5 Kalmer Ave., Apt. 13,Toronto

109 / Virgin / Cookshown / Russell Copeland, Newton Robinson

111 / Brampton / Brampton / Ernest Clarke, Brampton

132 / Joshua / Amberley / Charles Emmerton, RR 1, Kincardine

140 /   Smith / Baxter / Wesley Ruddick, RR. 1, Angus

148 / Duke of York / Hamilton / A.E. Hirst, 195 Rebecca St., Hamilton

159 / Arbah / St. Catherines / B. Houseburger, Jordan Station

161 / Jubilee / Clinton / H. Watkins, Goderich

269 / Elliott / Sault Ste. Marie / Burton J. Baker, 113 Curtis St., St. Thomas

278 / King Hiram / St. Thomas / Burton J. Baker, 113 Curtis St., St. Thomas

282 / Victoria / Markdale / I.T. Stoddart, Markdale

292 / The Temple / Toronto / Thomas Callon, 15 Gamble Ave., Toronto

297 / King Hirma / Mono Mills / Kenneth Baker, Caledon

301 / Carmel / Sarnia / John Morrison, 519 Devine St., Sarnia

302 / Mystic / Goodwood / D. Specley, Goodwood

335 / Red Cross Temple / Fordwick / Raymond Hill, RR 1, Wroxeter

337 / Maple Leaf / Toronto / John G. Guppy, 5 Moreland Rd., Toronto

342 / Red Cross / Toronto / J.F. White, Toronto

343 / Osprey / Feversham / Victor Wright, Feversham

344 / King Solomon / Toronto / Harry Steenson, 675 Glenore Ave., Toronto

345 / Mahood / Wallaceburg / Louis Turner, 312 Queen St., Wallaceburg

346 / Covenant / London / W.R. McFadden, 60 Wilson Ave., London

364 / Undivided Trinity / Brantford / Samuel Anderson, 217 Marlboro St., Brantford

365 / Laurel / Laurel / W.J. Lanktree, Laurel

384 / North Star / Collingwood / Harry J. Bell, Collingwood

403 / Jasper / Palgrave / A. McClean, Palgrave

418 / Golden Link / Gravenhurst / L. E. Jones, Gravenhurst

419 / Owen Sound / Owen Sound / William Bishop, Owen Sound

420 / Victory / Toronto / A. Kelly, 261 Westward Hoe, Toronto

429 / Broomhill / Petrolia / Ross Douglas, Petrolia

434 / Meaford / Meaford / D. Almond, Meaford

436 / Tara / Tara / James W. Sparling, Tara

454 / Peace / Welland / Otto More, Wellandport

539 / Windsor / Windsor / G.C. Bott, La Salle

551 / Guysboro / Simcoe / John Moore, Port Rowan

552 / Midland / Midland / Herbert A. Wales, Midland

601 / Allandale / Barrie / H. Green, 72 Campbell Ave., Barrie

603 / Huntsville / Huntsville / Roy Watt, Kearney

604 / Johnston of Ballykilbeg / Dunchurch / Percy Whitnell, Dunchurch

615 / Black Diamond / Goldsmith / F. Armstrong, RR 1, Staples

621 / Orangeville / Orangeville / W.E. Prior, Orangeville

660 / Liberty / Fort William / Samuel Millar, Port Arthur

679 / Wallace / Toronto / W.C. Harvey, 87 Hillsdale Ave., Toronto

686 / York / Toronto / W. C. Harvey, 59 Devon Rd., Toronto

695 / Couchiching / Orillia / Bert Harper, Orillia

712 / Grand Valley / Grand Valley / H. Crane, Grand Valley

739 / Orville / Orville / George Devitt, Parry Sound

757 / Pride of Middlesex / Guysboro / Frank Allright, Staffordville

758 / Beeton / Tottenham / H.O. Pattterson, Tottenham

759 / Thornbury / Thornbury / Alexander Gilroy, Clarksburg

761 / Diamond / Listowel / Kenneth Elliott, Listowel

762 / King Hiram / North Bay / George Stuart, 339 Lakeshore Drive, North Bay

763 / The Chosen Few / Oshawa / C.H. Doughton, 81 Roxborough Ave., Oshawa

771 / Golden Crown / Erie Richard Awde, Hagersville

775 / Forest / Forest / W.F. Freele, Forest

797 / Wingham / Wingham / George A. Brooks, RR 1,Wingham

805 / McCormack / Toronto / F. Clipperfield, 122 Ellins Ave., Toronto

820 / Lundy's Lane / Niagara Falls / Frank Fox, 2270 Kerr St., Niagara Falls

832 / Classic City / Stratford / William Carruthers, Stratford

833 / King Edward / Shelburne / Warner Allen, Hornings Mills

834 / Inniskilling / London / William Hodgson, 714 Waterloo St., London

835 / Northern Star / Beaverton / George Brotherson, Beaverton

842 / Bethany / Weston / J.B. Plunkett, RR 3, Woodbridge

846 / Excelsior / Toronto / J.R. Lockie, 54 Galt Ave., Toronto

847 / Pride of Manitoulin / Little Current / W.L. Everett, Little Current

848 / Englehart / Englehart / W. H. Swayne, New Liskeard

870 / Ulster / Toronto / Fred Wagg, 327 Booth Ave., Toronto

872 / Sudbury / Sudbury / R.J. LaSalle, Sudbury

877 / Olive Branch / Guelph / John Given, Guelph

895 / Harnby / Harnby / J. Graham, Milton

897 / Caleb's Royal Line / Toronto / Jack Marshall, 970 Eastern Ave., Toronto

904 / Woodham / Woodham / George Davis, Exeter

906 / Clougher / Clougher / Clyne Dobbs, Glencairn

910 / Bracebridge / Bracebridge / Henry Cole, Bracebridge

911 / Wood / Dunnville / B.R. Burgess, 2 Diltz Rd., Dunnville

912 / Lord Erne / Chatham / G. Lennox, Chatham

926 / Oxford / Tilsonburg / S. Sergeant, Tilsonburg

932 / Dundas / Dundas / W. H. Drummond, RR 1, Waterdown

935 / King Solomon / Woodstock / A. C. Evans, 308 Simcoe St.,Woodstock

937 / King Solomon / London / Harold J. Warner, 133 Main St., London

940 / Pride of the West / Eddy's Mills / Andrew Thompson, RR 1, Oil Springs

947 / Vimy Ridge / Fort Erie / M.A. Sayler, 228 Main St., Fort Erie

950 / Maple Leaf / Preston / Caleb Evans, 148 Norfolk Ave., Galt

951 / Canada / Iroquois Falls / R.J. Connelly, Iroquois Falls

959 / Pride of the North / Cochrane / T.J. Thompson, Cochrane

971 / Victory / Mount Forest / C. Daley, Mount Forest

974 / Mansfield / Mansfield / Melvin Gilroy, RR 3, Alliston

1025 / Diamond / Varna / Minion W. Heard, RR 2, Clinton

1027 / Lake St. Barnard / South River / Ralph Dodds, Golden Valley

1035 / Appin / Appin / George E. May, Appin

1054 / Palmerston / Palmerston / C.L. Foulston, RR 3, Palmerston

1058 / The Jewel / Chesley / Fred Bruegemann, 7th Ave., Hanover

1061 / Aurora / Aurora / J.W. Hirst, RR 1, Keswick

1090 / Wilkesport / Wilkesport / Gordon Bicum, RR 1, Sombra

1091 / Tuxia / Dundalk / William J. Nixon, RR 1, Picton Station

1092 / Joshua / Mimico / C.W. Waterhouse, 11 Flemington Rd., Toronto

1115 / Port Credit / Port Credit / W.A. Kennedy, 1149 Stratley Ave., Port Credit

1130 / Lion's Head / Lion's Head / Gerald Bell, Lion's Head

1151 / Friends of Ulster / Creemore / Allan Ritchie, RR Creemore

1163 / Saugeen / Varney / John McGirr, RR 4, Durham

1185 / Sir Henry Wilson / Arthur / M. McMullan, Arthur

1202 / Burning Bush / Toronto / M. Clarke, 3802 Bathurs St., Toronto

1204 / Ulster / Hamilton / Edward Rasperry, RR 3, Hannon

1226 / Rising Star / Blythe / Harvey Jacklin, RR 1, Ethel

1242 / Kirkland Lake / Kirkland Lake / E. Church, 34 Queen St., Kirkland Lake

1309 / Sutton / Sutton /

Provincial Jurisdiction of Eastern Ontario

115 / Victoria / Smith's Falls / Edwin Bradford, 19 King St. , Smith's Falls

167 / Queensborough / Queensborough / Allan McCoy, RR 3 Madoc

227 / City of Ottawa / Ottawa / A..C. Farquaharson, RR 2, Alymer

233 / King Edward VII / Perth / R.E. Sargent, Perth

261 / Weir / Peterborough / R/E/ Langley, RR 4 ,Peterborough

262 / Victoria / Lindsay / Norman Jewell, 7 Sussex St., Lindsay

293 / Queen Alexandria / Port Hope / N. Bolton, RR 1, Cobourg

311 / Norwood / Norwood / Gordon Stevenson, RR 2, Norwood

347 / Prince Edward / Picton / W.L. MacDonald, Picton

382 / Mispah / Foxboro / Garfield Evans, RR 5, Belleville

383 / Covenant / Brockville / Harry Anderson, Lynn

398 / Devotts / Blackstock / Leslie Brooks, Bowmanville

433 / Carp / Carp / Harold Miller, Carp

442 / Star of the East / Kemptville / Stanley Anderson, Oxford Station

509 / Prince Edward / Winchester / W.J. L. Boyd, Winchester

537 / Harmony / Lyndhurst / Bland Love, Lyndhurst

600 / Haliburton / Haliburton / Alfred Burke, Haliburton

614 / Bancroft / Bancroft / E.R. Wannamaker, Bancroft

617 / Brighton / Brighton / Frank Wilce, Colborne

625 / King Edward / Omemee / T.J. Payne, Omemee

631 / Frankfort / Frankford / Laurence Conley, RR 4, Frankford

639 / Carleton Place / Carleton Place / Keith Hobbs, RR 1, Ashton

696 / Mount Carmel / Shawville (Quebec) / William Pine, Shawville

697 / King Solomon / Lakefiled / K.C. Darling, RR 2, Lakefield

714 / Madoc / Madoc / Ken Gordon, Madoc

725 / John W. Bell / Centreville / James Hughes, Centreville

747 / Wellmans / Wellmans / Lorne White, Sterling

748 / Golden Star / Marmona / Gordon McFarlin, Marmora

754 / Rahab / North Gower / Edwin Hunt, RR 2, Osgoode

770 / Carmel / W. Huntingdon / Russell Sills, Ivanhoe, West Huntingdon

773 / Frontenac / Kingston / A.J. Johnston, 47 Point Cresent, RR 7 Kingston

776 / Richmond / Richmond / John Eadie, 551 Edison Ave., Ottawa

779 / King Edward / Minden / John Hounsell, Miners Bay

853 / Belleville / Belleville / Robert Ostofi, RR 3, Belleville

854 / Dunsford / Dunsford / W.W. Thurston, RR 2, Dunsford

863 / King George / Toledo / C.W. Sands, Frankville

878 / Trent Valley / Trenton / James A. Thompson, 53a Bay St., Trenton

883 / Patricia / New Dublin / Elmer Burnham, New Dublin

887 / Ulster Covenant / Monkland / Francis Revere, Monkland

896 / Eady / Eganville / Charles Sutton, RR 3, Pembroke

930 / King George / Wellington / Harry Wasmund, Wellington

933 / Cassburn / Cassburn / Malcolm McRae, Vankleek Hill, Cassburn

938 / Olive Leaf / Russell / R.E. Morrow, RR 2, Russell

944 / Forest Mills / Forest Mills / Stewart Dafoe, Lonsdale

945 / Pride of Cavan / Millbrook / H. Elgar, Millbrook

946 / Havelock / Havelock / Frank Elmhurst, RR 3, Havelock

949 / Bobcaygeon / Fenelon Falls / David Schell, Bobcaygeon

958 / Kirkfield / Kirkfield / William Brotherson, RR 1, Kirkfield

1047 / Acacia / Westboro / Ken Sparling, 188 Macy Boulevard, West Boro

1055 / Eldorado / Eldorado / Everett Defoe, Millbridge

1119 / Emerald / Kinburn / Delmar Baird, Kinburn

1132 / Trinity / Pembroke / George Matheson, RR 1, Pembroke

1165 / King Edward / Moulinette / Charles Fenton, 24 Bethune St., Long Sault

Provincial Jurisdiction of New Brunswick

62 / The Queen's / Lancaster / John Hall, Apihagui, King's Co.

305 / King's / Woodstock / Reid Kennedy, Debec

308 / White Stone / Fredericton / H.Ray Parent, 320 Sunset Drive, Fredericton

507 / Trinity / Saint John / Frank Ross, 11 Holland St., Saint John

520 / Olive Branch / Moncton / S. Blaine Perry, 181 High St., Moncton

680 / St. Stephen / St. Stephen / Wilmot Jamieson, St. Stephen

737 / Red Cross / Canterbury / Stewart Wright, Canterbury

880 / Hiram / Sussex / Frederick Kilpatrick, Sussex Corner

886 / Cromwell / Campbelltown / C.R. Sharpe, 214 Rosebury St., Campbelltown

888 / Faithview / Tracy Station / G.H. Bagley, 332 Forbes St., Fredericton

899 / Welsford / Welsford / Leslie Brundage, Oak Point, Welsford

909 / Riverview / Chipman / Ernest Sypher, Newcastle Creek

1028 / Kitchener / McKinleyville / W.J. Cleveland, Millerton

Provincial Jurisdiction of Nova Scotia

117 / Johnston / Halifax / S. Meservey, 66 Windsor St. Halifax

294 / Springhill / Springhill / Burton Vance, Mountain Road, Springhill

341 / Inniskilling / North Sydney / William Lowe, Clifford St., North Sydne

358 / Golden Star / Glace Bay / A.A. Stevens, 352 King Edward St., Glace Bay

519 / Rising Sun / New Glasgow / James Rodgers, 85 Elm St., New Glasgow

567 / Edward VII / Westville / Wilson Spencer , Westville

678 / Iron City / Whitney Pier (Sydney) / Paul W. Skanes, 41 Wesley St., Whitney Pier

865 / Sceptre / Lunenburg / E.H. Miller, Lunenburg

1245 / New Aberdeen / New Aberdeen / Herbert Chant, 7 Essex St., Glace Bay

1275 / Alexander McIntosh / Richmond / Theodore Fisher, RR 1, Malagash, Cumberland Co.

Provincial Jurisdiction of Newfoundland

216 / Rose of Sharon / St. John's / William Le Grow, 12 Howlett Ave., St. John's

361 / Olive Branch / Burin / Leonard V. Beasley / Burin

458 / Lily of the Valley / Bay Roberts / Samuel Dawe, Coley's Point, Bay Roberts

514 / Pretoria / Carbonear / William J. Moore, Carbonear

546 / Bright and Morning Star / Heart's Content / Herbert Bryant, Heart's Content

566 / Duke of York / Western Bay / Harold Pennell, Cohoe Point, Cove

647 / William Johnston / Greenspond / Alexander White, Greenspond

648 / Gushne / Wesleyville / Raymond Parsons, Wesleyville

650 / Trinity / Port Rexton / Baxter J. Barbour, Port Rexton

703 / Bethel / Twilingate / Ronald Sharpe, Twilingate

704 / Lily of the North / Beaumont / T.H. Short, Beaumont

729 / John Knox / Grand Bank / Harold Rideout, Grand Bank

753 / Pansy / Lewisporte / Herbert Freake, Lewisporte

772 / Dreadnought / Bonavista / George Hicks. Bonavista

787 / King George V / Broadcove / Warren Hudson, Broadcove

789 / Clarke Wallace / New Harbour / Clyde Higdon, New Harbout

791 / Sunrise / Porte de Grave / Harrison Ralph, Porte de Grave

818 / Prince Edward / Lower Island Cove / Arthur Champion, Lower Island Cove

821 / Ark of Safety / Spaniard's Bay / George E. Drover, Spaniard's Bay

830 / Excelsior / Catalina / Clayton Johnston, Catalina

837 / Coronation / Hant's Harbour / Reginald Penny, Hant's Harbour

838 / Jethro / Perry's Cove / George King, Perry's Cove

851 / Sunbeam / Coley's Point / Clifton Batten, Coley's Point

867 / Rainbow / Kelligrews / Alexander Tilley, Kelligrews

869 / Livingstone / Brigus / C.N. Percy / Brigus

876 / Terra Nova / Fogo / Uriah Hewitt, Fogo

879 / St. Barbes / Bonne Bay / E.G. Howell, Woody Point

900 / Fern / Grand Falls / W.H. Moore, Grand Falls

915 / Mountjoy / St. George's / Chester Tilley, St. George's

923 / Earl of Erne / Cupids / Wilfred Whelan, Cupids

927 / Lord Robert / Little Bay Island / Gerald Wiseman, Little Bay Island

934 / Caribou Hill / Herring Neck / George Mills, Herring Neck

941 / Kitchener / Trinity / Cyril Bartlett, Trinity

943 / Liberty / Pouch Cove / Paul Moore, Pouch Cove

960 / Glad Tidings / Upper Island Cove / Max Drover, Upper Island Cove

966 / Beaumont Hamwell / Foxtrap / Charles Batten, Foxtrap

973 / Juniper Brook / Garnish / Isaac Barnes, Garnish

983 / Prince John / Fortune / Fred Lake, Fortune

984 / Oleanda / Botwood / C.J. Elliott, Botwood

985 / Bishop Jones / Salvage / Gordon J. Dyke, Salvage

986 / Star of the East / Moreton's Harbour / Stewart Taylor, Moreton's Harbour

1030 / Primrose / Winterton / George White, Winterton

1049 / Earl Kitchener / St. Anthony / Albert Richard, St. Anthony

1050 / Enterprise / Kingwell / Jesse Slade, Kingwell

1062 / Fosters Point / Fosters Point / A. Strong, Foster's Point

1064 / Lord Kitchener / New Perlican / Charles Warren, New Perlican

1093 / Clarenville / Clarenville / Frederick Balson, Clarenville

1114 / The North / Lance au Claire / Raymond Letto, Lance au Claire

1116 / Verner / Petries / Edward Buffett, Curling

1117 / Britannia / Britannia / William Walters, Petley

1129 / Gallipoli / Old Perlican / William Squires, Old Perlican

1152 / Norris Point / Norris Point / Michael Organ, Norris Point

1153 / Donald Morrison / Green's Harbour / Stanley Brace, Green's Harbour

1161 / Bennett / Channel / R.F. Billiard, Channel

1166 / Mount Carmel / Humber Mouth / Jacob Morgan, Humber Mouth

1181 / Black Rock / Port Elizabeth / J.J. Senior, Port Elizabeth

1200 / Caville / Gambo / Harold Paul, Dark Cove, Gambo

1201 / White Lily / Brownsdale / George Austin, Brownsdale

1215 / Hillview / Hillview / Edward Smith, Hillview

1216 / Excelsior / Little Heart's Ease / Cecil Stringer, Little Heart's Ease

1225 / Langmead / Bishop's Falls / James E. Coffin, Bishop's Falls

1229 / Buchans / Buchans / Jacob Killoway, Buchans

1230 / Springdale / Springdale / Frederick Jenkins, Springdale

1231 / Red Bay / Red Bay, Labrador / Reginald Moore, Red Bay, Labrador

1241 / Corner Brook / Corner Brook / Clayton Hull, 51 Greenings Hill, Cornerbrook

1243 / Nippers Harbour / Nippers Harbour / Earl E. Noble, Nippers Harbour

1244 / Gaultois / Gaultois / Edgar Green, Gaultois

1246 / Hermitage / Hermitage / Stanley Roberts, Hermitage

1247 / Joe Batt's Arm / Joe Batt's Arm / Alexander Hewitt, Joe Batt's Arm

1248 / Musgravetown / Musgravetown / Lloyd Simmons, Musgravetown

1249 / Bell Island / Bell Island / Leonard Gosse, Bell Island

1250 / Clark's Beach / Clark's Beach / Everit Reid, Clark's Beach

1251 / Burgeo / Burgeo / Lot Cossar, Burgeo

1253 / Burnside / Burnside / Augustus Oldford, Burnside

1254 / Seldom Come Bye / Seldom Come Bye / Christopher Boone, Seldom Come Bye

1255 / Carmanville / Carmanville / Edwin Easton, Noggin Cove

1256 / Hillgrade / Hillgrade / Junior Ings, Fairbanks

1257 / Whitebourne / Whitebourne / C.R. Moore, Whitebourne

1258 / Bauline / Bauline / Ambrose King, Bauline

1259 / Shearstown / Shearstown / Victor Mercer, Shearstown

1261 / Musgrave Harbour / Musgrave Harbour / E.G. Abbott, Musgrave Harbour

1262 / Bunyan's Cove / Bunyan's Cove / Maxwell Oldford, Bunyan's Cove

1263 / Fair Island / Fair Island / Manuel Rogers, Fair Island

1264 / Harry's Harbour / Harry's Harbour / Jackson England, Harry's Harbour

1265 / Portugal Cove / Portugal Cove / Gordon Allen, Portugal Cove

1266 / Princeton / Princeton / S.J. Prince, Princeton

1269 / Arnold's Cove / Arnold's Cove / Eugene Guy, Arnold's Cove

1270 / Bishop's Cove / Bishop's Cove / Walter Smith, Bishop's Cove

1271 / Heart's Delight / Heart's Delight / Denziel J. Hannm, Heart's Delight

1272 / Change Islands / Change Islands / Lester Diamond, Change Islands

1273 / Chamberlains / Chamberlains / Ronald Smith, Chamberlains

1276 / Norman's Cove / Norman's Cove / Ernest Newhook, Norman's Cove

1277 / Harbor Grace / Harbor Grace / George R. Pike, Harbor Grace

1278 / Happy Adventure / Happy Adventure / George Mathen, Happy Adventure

1279 / St. Philips / St. Philips / Clive Tucker, St. Philips

1280 / Codroy / Codroy / George Frander, Codroy

1282 / Rose Blanche / Rose Blanche / Albert Harwood, Rose Blanche

1283 / Deer Lake / Deer Lake / William Hutchcroft, Deer Lake

1284 / Hopewell / Hopewell / Aubrey Dawe, Upper Guilies

1285 / Creston / Creston / Joseph Mays, Creston

1286 / Lumsden / Lumsden / Wilson Parson, Lumsden

1287 / Great Brehat / Great Brehat / Wallace Ward, Great Brehat

1288 / Old Shop / Old Shop / Stanley Dawe, Old Shop

1289 / Gander Bay / Gander Bay / Frank Head, Gander Bay

1290 / Poole Island / Poole Island / Frank kelloway, Poole Island

1291 / Gander / Gander / Herbert Toms, Gander

1292 / La Scie / La Scie / Arthur Richards, La Scie

1293 / Glovertown / Glovertown / Herbert Feltham, Glovertown

1294 / Hare Bay / Hare Bay / Eli West, Glovertown

1295 / Isle Aux Morts / Isle Aux Morts / Melvin Bragg, Isle Aux Morts

1298 / Victoria Cove / Victoria Cove / Lester King, Victoria Cove

1299 / Woody Island / Woody Island / Chesley Piercey, Woody Island

1300 / Lark Harbour / Lark Harbour / H. R. Shepherd, Lark Harbour

1301 / Lethbridge / Lethbridge / Naaman J. Lane, Lethbridge

1303 / Summerville / Summerville / Naaman J. Lane, Lethbridge

1304 / Port Blandford / Port Blandford / Hector Greenins, Port Blandford

1305 / Bay L'Argent / Bay L'Argent / E. Le Grow, Bay L'Argent

1306 / Wareham / Wareham / Ronald Hunt, Wareham

1307 / St. Jones Within / St. Jones Within / Benoni Robbins, Herbert Cove

1308 / Dover B.B / Dover B.B. / John Noble, Dover

Preceptories in Province of Quebec

155 / Knights of Ulster / Montreal / A.D. Sharkey, 2287 Old Orchard Ave., Montreal

1224 / Hiram / Montreal / C.G. Clifford, 3343 Wellingston St., Verdun

1267 / Harrington / Harrington / Scott McLean, RR 2, Calumet

Preceptories in Prince Edward Island

192 / Pinette / Pinette / Clarence R. McKenzie, Beatons Mills

905 / Abegweit / Kingston / L.S. Seaman, Kingston

936 / King Hiram / Central Bedeque / T.J. Inman, RR 3, Summerside

1296 / Coleman / Coleman / David Lockhart, Coleman

1302 / Charlottetown / Charlottetown /

5. APPENDIX "B" - Church Service with Royal Black Knights at St. James Presbyterian Church, Truro, Nova Scotia, November 3, 1929

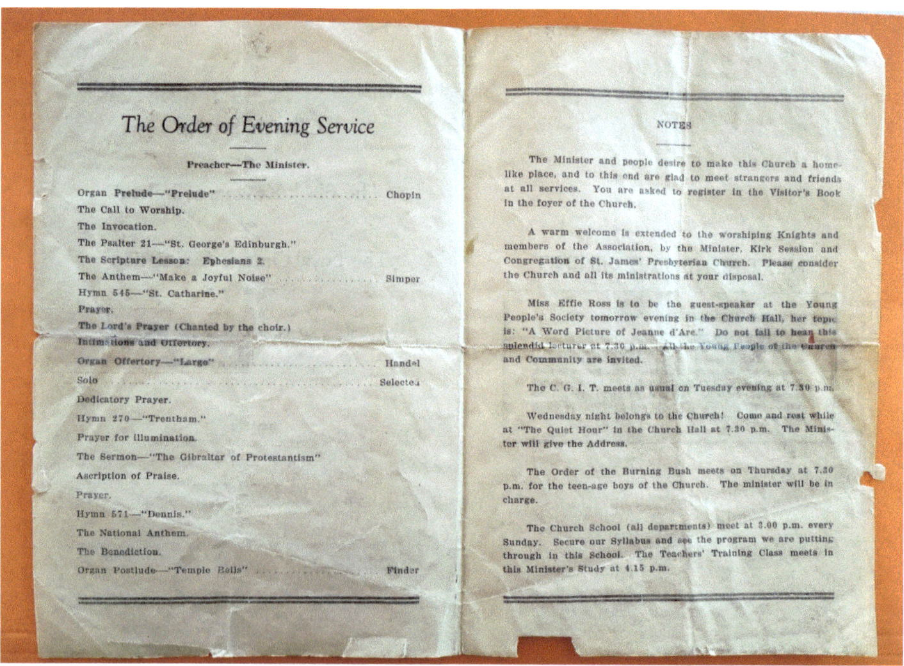

The Order of Evening Service

Preacher—The Minister.

Organ Prelude—"Prelude" .... Chopin
The Call to Worship.
The Invocation.
The Psalter 21—"St. George's Edinburgh."
The Scripture Lesson: Ephesians 2.
The Anthem—"Make a Joyful Noise" .... Simper
Hymn 545—"St. Catharine."
Prayer.
The Lord's Prayer (Chanted by the choir.)
Intimations and Offertory.

Organ Offertory—"Large" .... Handel
Solo .... Selected
Dedicatory Prayer.
Hymn 270—"Trentham."
Prayer for Illumination.
The Sermon—"The Gibraltar of Protestantism"
Ascription of Praise.
Prayer.
Hymn 571—"Dennis."
The National Anthem.
The Benediction.
Organ Postlude—"Temple Bells" .... Finder

NOTES

The Minister and people desire to make this Church a home-like place, and to this end are glad to meet strangers and friends at all services. You are asked to register in the Visitor's Book in the foyer of the Church.

A warm welcome is extended to the worshiping Knights and members of the Association, by the Minister, Kirk Session and Congregation of St. James' Presbyterian Church. Please consider the Church and all its ministrations at your disposal.

Miss Effie Ross is to be the guest-speaker at the Young People's Society tomorrow evening in the Church Hall, her topic is: "A Word Picture of Jeanne d'Arc." Do not fail to hear this splendid lecturer at 7.30 p.m. All the Young People of the Church and Community are invited.

The C. G. I. T. meets as usual on Tuesday evening at 7.30 p.m.

Wednesday night belongs to the Church! Come and rest while at "The Quiet Hour" in the Church Hall at 7.30 p.m. The Minister will give the Address.

The Order of the Burning Bush meets on Thursday at 7.30 p.m. for the teen-age boys of the Church. The minister will be in charge.

The Church School (all departments) meet at 3.00 p.m. every Sunday. Secure our Syllabus and see the program we are putting through in this School. The Teachers' Training Class meets in this Minister's Study at 4.15 p.m.

6. APPENDIX " C " - Price List for Royal Black Knights

Price List continued

DRESS SASHES

No. 776A

REGULATION DESIGN

SASH—No. 776A—Heavy corded black moire ribbon with scarlet edge, emblems embroidered in full colour; trimmed with full pleated rosette at shoulder and join and non-tarnishable gold silk braid and heavy fringe.   **Each $18.45**

No. 778

SASH—No. 778—Black velvet, elaborately embroidered in coloured silks; bordered in red and gold, full pleated rosettes at shoulder and join; heavy gold silk braid and fringe as illustrated, fully lined and interlined.   **Each $30.25**

SASH—No. 779—Same design as No. 778, but with emblems hand embroidered in gold and silver bullion; trimmed with gold bullion fringe and braid.   **Each $55.00**

DOMINION REGALIA Limited   84 ELM ST., TORONTO, CANADA

ROYAL BLACK KNIGHT'S APRONS

No. 777

APRON—No. 777—Genuine white lambskin with emblems printed in black; trimmed with blue corded ribbon, fully lined, loose flap. **Each $8.25**

No. 780

APRON—No. 780—Dress Apron, white lambskin with emblems in full colour, trimmed with blue corded ribbon and gold silk braid and fringe, fully lined. **Each $11.30**

SPECIAL NOTICE

ALL THE ITEMS OF

PERSONAL REGALIA

SHOWN HERE ARE OF

"OFFICIAL" DESIGN

Manufactured by

DOMINION REGALIA Ltd.

under contract with the

Grand Black Chapter of B.A.

and in support of the

Grand Black Chapter's

"Dress Up The Black"

Campaign

ORDER DIRECT

from

Dominion Regalia Ltd.

84 ELM ST.

Toronto   Canada

DOMINION REGALIA Limited

84 ELM ST., TORONTO, CANADA

WEDGE CAP   No. 990—As illustrated on front cover, has black sides, red top, white trim and metal triangle cap badge. **Each**   **$2.25**
Per doz. $24.00

PARADE TIE   No. 991—Of lustrous black satin with emblematic design in colour. **Each**   **$1.50**
Per doz. $16.50

EMBLEM PINS

No. 3—Metal gilt button enamelled in red. **Each $1.00**   **Per doz. $9.00**

No. 170B — Smaller size, with red enamelled finish and 10K gold quality. **Each $3.00**

No. 3

170B

10K GOLD RINGS

No. 689/22
In 10K Gold
Each $18.50

689/22

518/11

No. 518/11
In 10K Gold
Each $19.50

WRITE FOR RING SIZE CARD

ANY ITEM OF PERSONAL REGALIA IS A WORTHWHILE GIFT FOR:—

Christmas — Birthday — Anniversary

Presentation — or Special Occasion

- -

ORDER BLANK

NAME ....
(Print Clearly)

ADDRESS .... PROV. ....

ITEM No.	DESCRIPTION	PRICE

ALL SHIPMENTS WILL BE SENT C.O.D. POST or EXPRESS

Dominion Regalia Limited
84 ELM STREET, TORONTO

7. ABOUT THE AUTHOR

Brian McConnell, UE, B.A. (Hons) LL.B. is a retired lawyer, historian, genealogist and author. This is his 11th nonfiction history book. Some of his relatives immigrated to Canada from Ireland and were Royal Black Knights. He has been researching them for over 30 years and is the author of four other books which concern members of the Loyal Orange Association. These are: 1) The Royal Black Knights in Canada; 2) The L.O.B.A. in Canada; 3) The Grand Mistress and the Ladies Orange Benevolent Association; and 4) Loyal and True: Spurgeon L.O.L. # 1624.